Made Whole

Healing, Wholeness, and Holiness in a Sex-Saturated World

Companion Guide for Couples, Groups, and Group Leaders

Joshua & Hope Broome

Made Whole

Healing, Wholeness, and Holiness in a Sex-Saturated World

Companion Guide for Couples, Groups, and Group Leaders

Joshua & Hope Broome

PUBLISHING

Made Whole: Healing, Wholeness, and Holiness in a Sex-Saturated World: Companion Guide for Couples, Groups, and Group Leaders
Copyright © 2026 by XO Marriage

Scripture quotations taken from the Holy Bible, New International Version ®, NIV ® Copyright © 1973, 1978, 1984, 2011 by Biblica, Inc. Used with permission. All rights reserved worldwide.

All rights reserved. No portion of this publication may be reproduced, stored in a retrieval system, or transmitted in any form by any means—electronic, mechanical, photocopying, recording, or any other—without prior permission from the publisher.

ISBN: 978-1-960870-84-1 eBook
ISBN: 978-1-960870-85-8 Paperback

XO Marriage is a leading creator of relationship-based resources. We focus primarily on marriage-related content for churches, small group curriculum, and people looking for timeless truths about relationships and overall marital health. For more information on other resources from XO, visit xomarriage.com.

XO Marriage
1021 Grace Lane
Southlake, TX 76092

While the authors make every effort to provide accurate URLs at the time of printing for external or third-party internet websites, neither they nor the publisher assume any responsibility for changes or errors made after publication.

Printed in the United States of America

26 27 28 29—5 4 3 2 1

Table of Contents

Introduction

A Word from Joshua & Hope

Welcome to ***Made Whole.***

We are so honored to walk with you through these sessions. Our heart is simple: We want to help couples like you pursue purity, rebuild trust, strengthen intimacy, and live in holiness in a world discipled by lust.

Wherever you are in your story—whether you are healing from past sexual brokenness, fighting current battles, or simply wanting to build a marriage that is protected and thriving—you're not alone. And Jesus is not intimidated by anything you are walking through.

This course was born out of our own journey. We know what it is like to face the devastation of sexual sin. We understand what it is like to feel like there is no way forward. But we have also experienced the redemptive power of Jesus to see a marriage that was once shattered become stronger, deeper, and more honest than ever before.

That is what we want for you.

We believe every marriage today is living within a spiritual war zone. We don't mean that there is a war between husbands and wives; we are talking about weapons targeted directly at them. Pornography, comparison, secrecy, temptation—none of those are random struggles. They are strategic assaults on your intimacy, your unity, your covenant, and yes, your marriage. But we have some good news: Jesus can't be intimidated by any of it. And in Him, the ultimate victory has already been won.

What This Course Will Accomplish

Nothing we will say is intended to bring shame. We don't think behavior modification alone is the answer. We are going to tell you how your heart can be transformed. And we will boldly say that only Jesus can do that.

Here's what we want you to get out of this course:

- **To recognize the spiritual battle.**

  The enemy is targeting your marriage, not just your behavior.

- **To experience gospel hope.**
  The same Jesus who will forgive you can also restore you.
- **To learn to forgive and communicate.**
  Mercy and transparency are key to rebuilding trust.
- **To pursue redeemed intimacy.**
  You can come together again as one even in the middle of chaos.
- **To build practical rhythms.**
  We want to tell you how to build structures into your marriage that will protect it help you thrive together.

We would never promise that your marriage will become perfect. But we will tell you that it can be a place of healing, wholeness, and holiness, which will then be a testimony to the world of what covenant love looks like.

About This Study Guide Collection

To help you get the most out of this course, we have created three companion guides, and all three are in this book. Each one serves a different purpose, and together, they provide a complete experience:

- **The Couple's Discussion Guide** is for the two of you—just you and your spouse. These conversations go deeper than what is appropriate in a group setting. They are more personal, more vulnerable, and more specific to your unique marriage. Some of these questions might be hard. That is okay. Healing often happens in the uncomfortable places. Use this guide to have the conversations that really matter.
- **The Group Participant Guide** is designed for couples to journey together in community. There is something powerful about sitting with other couples who are fighting for their marriages too. You will find discussion questions, teaching notes, application challenges, and resources for deeper study. If you are in a hard season, you will discover you are not alone. If you are in a season of healing, you will be able to encourage others. Iron sharpens iron.
- **The Leader Guide** is for those brave souls who are stepping up to facilitate a group. Leading is not about having all the answers—it is about creating a safe space for couples to encounter God and each other. This guide includes facilitation tips, session-by-session notes, and resources for supporting group members who may be walking through crisis. If you are a leader, thank you. What you are doing matters more than you know.

We have also included some information for those who are walking through the pain of betrayal, separation, or divorce. Because here is the reality: Some of the people engaging with this material are in beautiful seasons of marriage, and some are barely holding on. Some may be separated. Some may be grieving a marriage that has been deeply wounded. We want everyone to find hope and healing, wherever they are.

A Personal Word from Us to You

Listen—no matter where you are in your marriage right now, **there is hope.**

Your marriage was not designed just to survive. In Christ, it was designed to thrive. Not because you are perfect, but because Jesus is faithful.

Healing is available. Wholeness is possible. Holiness is worth pursuing. Intimacy can be redeemed.

You are not too far gone. Your story is not over.

If you are in a beautiful season—keep giving God glory. If you are in a hard season—keep giving Him access. If you are in a healing season—keep giving Him time. If you are in a confused season—keep giving Him trust.

And remember: reaching out for help is not failure. Whether it is a pastor, a Christian counselor, or trusted friends—community is part of how God heals His people.

We are praying for you. We believe in what God is going to do in your marriage.

Let's grow together. Let's heal together. And let's pursue holiness, wholeness, and oneness—together.

In Christ,

Joshua & Hope Broome

Couple's Guide

A Note to Couples

This guide is designed for the two of you—just you and your spouse. We have placed this here so you can have deeper conversations than a group setting allows. These questions are more personal, more vulnerable, and more specific to your unique marriage.

Some of these conversations may be difficult. Healing often happens in the uncomfortable places. Approach each session with grace, curiosity, and a commitment to truly hear each other.

Because of the sensitive nature of this material, please remember: *this is not about blame. This is about healing together.* You are not enemies—you are teammates fighting a common enemy.

Guidelines for Your Conversations

- **Create sacred space.** Turn off your phones. Find a quiet place. Give each other your full attention. Consider lighting a candle or playing soft worship music to set the tone.
- **Listen to understand, not to respond.** Let your spouse finish their thoughts completely before you speak. Resist the urge to defend, explain, or fix.
- **Use "I" statements.** Say "I feel..." or "I need..." rather than "You always..." or "You never..." This keeps the conversation safe rather than accusatory.
- **Stay curious.** Ask follow-up questions. Seek to understand your spouse's heart. Say things like, "Help me understand..." or "Tell me more about that..."
- **Pray together.** Begin and end each conversation in prayer. You may not be used to doing that—this is a good opportunity to start.
- **Take breaks if needed.** If emotions run high, pause and return when you are both in a calmer place. It is okay to say, "I need a few minutes. Can we come back to this?"
- **Maintain confidentiality.** What is shared between you stays between you. This creates safety for vulnerability. You may need to talk to a counselor or

a pastor, but agree that you will not divulge your conversations to friends or family.

- **Extend grace.** Neither of you will do this perfectly. Assume the best about each other's intentions.
- **Celebrate progress.** Acknowledge when you have had a good conversation. Thank each other for being vulnerable. Small wins build momentum.

Couple's Session 1

The War for Holiness

"Put on the full armor of God, so that you can take your stand against the devil's schemes."

—Ephesians 6:11

Opening Prayer

Pray together:

Lord, we come before You acknowledging that our marriage is in a battle—not against each other, but against an enemy who wants to destroy us. Open our eyes to see what we have been blind to. Give us courage to be honest about our struggles. Help us to fight together, not against each other. We need Your strength, Your wisdom, and Your protection. In Jesus' name, Amen.

Scripture Meditation

Read these verses together and discuss what they reveal about the battle we face:

Ephesians 6:12:

For our struggle is not against flesh and blood, but against the rulers, against the authorities, against the powers of this dark world and against the spiritual forces of evil in the heavenly realms.

1 Peter 5:8:

Be alert and of sober mind. Your enemy the devil prowls around like a roaring lion looking for someone to devour.

What do these verses reveal about the nature of the battle? How does knowing your enemy help you fight more effectively?

Heart-to-Heart Questions

Use these questions to guide your conversation. Take your time with each one.

1. **Naming the Battle:** Where do you see the enemy targeting our marriage right now? Be specific and honest. (Pornography? Comparison? Secrecy? Emotional distance? Fantasy? Social media? Busyness that crowds out connection?) How long has this been a struggle?
2. **The Anatomy of Lust:** Joshua teaches that lust follows a pattern: desire → deception → disconnection. Where have you seen this pattern in your own life? Where have you seen it affecting our marriage? What "deceptions" have you believed?
3. **Secrecy Check:** On a scale of 1–10, how transparent have we been with each other about our struggles? What has kept us from being more honest? What fears do you have about being fully known?
4. **Digital Boundaries:** What digital boundaries do we currently have in place? What boundaries do we need to establish or strengthen? How do you feel about accountability software, shared passwords, or device-free zones?
5. **Fighting Together:** How can we better fight this battle together rather than alone? What does it look like for us to be on the same team? What do you need from me when you are tempted?
6. **Hope Check:** Do you believe our marriage can become "stronger, deeper, and more honest than ever before"? What gives you hope? What makes you doubt?

Reflection: Our Battle Plan

Take turns completing these statements:

"One area where I need to close the door to secrecy is ____________________."

"One way I want you to fight alongside me is ____________________________."

"One thing I am committed to doing differently is _________________________."

Journaling Prompts

Spend 5–10 minutes journaling individually, then share what you wrote:

- What fears have kept me from being fully honest about my struggles?
- Where have I believed the enemy's lies about my marriage or my spouse?
- What would change if we truly fought this battle together?

Going Deeper Exercise: Battle Station

Together, create a "Battle Station" for your marriage—a list of resources and practices you will use when temptation or struggle hits:

- Scripture we will memorize: ____________________
- Person we will call for accountability: ____________________
- Prayer we will pray together: ____________________
- Worship music we will play: ____________________
- Physical action we will take (walk, exercise, etc.): ____________________

Write this down and put it somewhere you can both access quickly.

This Week's Commitment

Establish a Digital Boundary Rule

Together, establish digital boundaries for your home. Write your decisions below:

Device location: Where will devices stay at night? ____________________

Accountability: What accountability measures will we put in place? ____________________

Outside accountability partner: Husband: ____________________
Wife: ____________________

Weekly check-in: Day: ____________________ Time: ____________________

Weekly Check-In Questions

Come back to these questions mid-week:

- How did I do at walking in the light this week?
- What triggered temptation for me?
- Where did I see you fighting for our marriage?

Closing: United in Battle

Stand facing each other. Hold hands. Look into each other's eyes.

Take turns saying: "I commit to fighting for our marriage by ____________________."

Then pray together:

Lord, we are in this battle together. Help us fight side by side. Give us wisdom to build boundaries that protect our marriage. Give us courage to be honest. Give us grace when we fail. We trust You. In Jesus' name, Amen.

Couple's Session 2

The Gospel and the Wounds of Betrayal

"Create in me a pure heart, O God, and renew a steadfast spirit within me. Restore to me the joy of your salvation."

—Psalm 51:10, 12

Opening Prayer

Pray together:

Father, we bring our wounds to You. Some of them are fresh. Some of them are old but still hurt. We ask for Your healing presence in this conversation. Give us the grace to be honest, the courage to confess, and the strength to forgive. Help us to see each other the way You see us—not as enemies, but as beloved children in need of Your grace. In Jesus' name, Amen.

Scripture Meditation

Read these verses together and discuss what they reveal about confession, forgiveness, and restoration:

2 Corinthians 7:10:

Godly sorrow brings repentance that leads to salvation and leaves no regret, but worldly sorrow brings death.

1 John 1:9:

If we confess our sins, he is faithful and just and will forgive us our sins and purify us from all unrighteousness.

What is the difference between godly sorrow and worldly sorrow? What does true confession look like?

Heart-to-Heart Questions

Use these questions to guide your conversation. Take your time. Some of these may require pause and prayer.

1. **The Weight of Wounds:** Is there any pain or betrayal in our marriage that we have not fully addressed? What do you need me to understand about how you have been hurt? What has been the hardest part of this for you?
2. **Worldly Sorrow vs. Godly Repentance:** When I have hurt you, have my apologies felt like worldly sorrow ("I'm sorry I got caught") or godly repentance (true ownership, honesty, and change)? How can I do better?
3. **The Four Stages:** Hope teaches that trust is rebuilt through Honesty → Consistency → Safety → Intimacy. Where are we in this process? Which stage needs the most attention right now?
4. **Creating Safety:** Do you feel safe asking me questions about my struggles without being shamed, dismissed, or met with defensiveness? What would help you feel safer?
5. **Boundaries vs. Bitterness:** Are there boundaries we need to establish for our healing? What is the difference between healthy boundaries and punishing walls? How can we hold both forgiveness and boundaries at the same time?
6. **Gospel Hope:** What would it look like for our marriage to be "stronger, deeper, and more honest than ever before"? What gives you hope that this is possible?

Healing Exercise: Truth + Grace

If there is a specific hurt that needs to be addressed, use this framework:

- **The one who caused hurt:** *"Here is what happened.* [Be specific—facts first.] *Here is why I made those choices.* [Be honest about the heart issue.] *Here is how I am taking responsibility so it never happens again.* [Be concrete about the plan.] Will you forgive me?"
- **The one who was hurt:** *"I forgive you.* [This is a decision, not a feeling.] *I am choosing to release this. I am committed to walking through the healing process with you."*
- **Together:** *"Jesus, we bring this to You. Heal what has been broken. Restore what has been lost. We trust You with our healing."*

Journaling Prompts

Spend 5-10 minutes journaling individually, then share what you wrote:

- What wounds have I been carrying that I have not fully shared?
- Where do I need to move from worldly sorrow to godly repentance?
- What would it take for me to truly trust again?

Going Deeper Exercise: The Release

Write down on separate pieces of paper:

- Hurts I have been holding onto
- Ways I have contributed to our brokenness
- Fears about our healing process

Pray together and symbolically release these papers to God. You might tear them up, burn them safely, or simply set them aside as a declaration that you are letting go.

This Week's Commitment: The Truth + Grace Table

Practice the Truth + Grace Table this week:

- Set aside 15-20 minutes to sit together, face to face.
- Each spouse shares one truth: "What hurt me?" or "What temptation surfaced?"
- Each spouse shares one grace: "What is God teaching me?" or "Where do I see hope?"
- Close in prayer together.

Our Truth + Grace Table time will be: Day ___________ Time ____________

Weekly Check-In Questions

Come back to these questions mid-week:

- How am I doing at practicing godly repentance rather than worldly sorrow?
- What is one way I saw you working toward our healing this week?
- Where do I still need to grow in creating safety for you?

Closing: Hope for Healing

Look into each other's eyes. Take turns saying:

"One thing that gives me hope for our healing is ______________________."

"I am committed to walking this journey with you because ______________."

Close in prayer together.

Couple's Session 3

Covenant Forgiveness and Communication

"Be kind and compassionate to one another, forgiving each other, just as in Christ God forgave you."

—Ephesians 4:32

Opening Prayer

Pray together:

Father, forgiveness is hard. Communication is hard. But we know that where forgiveness opens the heart, communication can rebuild trust. Soften our hearts today. Help us to listen without defending. Help us to speak truth seasoned with grace. Where walls have been built, tear them down. Where patterns have been destructive, give us new ways. In Jesus' name, Amen.

Scripture Meditation

Read these verses together and discuss what they reveal about forgiveness and communication:

James 1:19:

Everyone should be quick to listen, slow to speak and slow to become angry.

Colossians 3:13:

Bear with each other and forgive one another if any of you has a grievance against someone. Forgive as the Lord forgave you.

What does it mean to be "quick to listen"? How did the Lord forgive us, and what does it mean to forgive that way?

Heart-to-Heart Questions

Use these questions to guide your conversation.

1. **The Work of Forgiveness:** Is there any forgiveness work that still needs to begin in our marriage? What is keeping us from forgiving fully? What would it take for you to truly release this?
2. **Listening vs. Defending:** When we have conflict, do I tend to listen or defend? How does that make you feel? What would help me become a better listener?
3. **Safe Topics:** What topics still feel unsafe for us to discuss? Why do you think that is? What would need to change for those topics to feel safer?
4. **Confession Framework:** Joshua teaches to share facts first, emotions second, and plan for change last. How can we practice this? When I confess something, what do you need to hear from me?
5. **Empathy Check:** On a scale of 1–10, how well do I show empathy when you are hurting? What does empathy look like to you? What do I do that feels empathetic? What feels dismissive?
6. **Our Communication Patterns:** What communication patterns did we each bring from our families of origin? Which are helpful? Which are harmful? What new patterns do we want to create?

Reflection: Truth Rhythms Builder

Discuss what "truth rhythms" you want to build into your marriage:

- **Confession:** We will practice proactive honesty by ____________________
- **Gratitude:** We will express specific thankfulness at ____________________
- **Prayer:** We will pray together at ___________ for ___________________minutes
- **Affirmation:** We will speak words of life by ____________________
- **Boundaries:** We will adjust or reinforce these boundaries as needed: ____________________

Journaling Prompts

Spend 5–10 minutes journaling individually, then share what you wrote:

- What makes me defensive when we talk about hard things?
- Where have I withheld forgiveness, and what is it costing our marriage?
- What would our communication look like if we were both "quick to listen"?

Going Deeper Exercise: Role Reversal

Take turns speaking from your spouse's perspective. Complete these sentences as if you were your spouse:

- "When we have conflict, I feel ____________________."
- "What I wish my spouse understood about me is ____________________."
- "The way I feel most loved is ____________________."

Discuss: How accurate was your spouse's understanding of you? What surprised you?

This Week's Commitment: Nightly Practice

Begin a simple five-minute nightly practice. Each night, before bed, ask each other:

- "Did I live in the light today?" (This invites honesty and confession.)
- "How can I serve you tomorrow?" (This invites humility and partnership.)

Track your nightly practice this week:

Day 1: ____________________

Day 2: ____________________

Day 3: ____________________

Day 4: ____________________

Day 5: ____________________

Day 6: ____________________

Day 7: ____________________

Weekly Check-In Questions

Come back to these questions mid-week:

- How did I do at listening without defending this week?
- Where did I see you practicing empathy?
- What is one thing I am grateful for about how we communicated?

Closing: Gratitude Exchange

Look into each other's eyes. Take turns saying:

"I am grateful for the way you ____________________."

"One thing I love about how you communicate is ____________________."

Close in prayer together.

Couple's Session 4

Redeemed Intimacy

"The two will become one flesh. So they are no longer two, but one flesh."

—Mark 10:8

Opening Prayer

Pray together:

Father, You designed intimacy. You called it good. But life has a way of stealing what You intended to be beautiful. Redeem our intimacy—emotionally, spiritually, and physically. Help us to pursue oneness even in the midst of chaos. Heal what has been broken. Restore what has been lost. Make our marriage a place where intimacy thrives. In Jesus' name, Amen.

Scripture Meditation

Read these verses together and discuss what they reveal about God's design for intimacy:

Genesis 2:24–25:

That is why a man leaves his father and mother and is united to his wife, and they become one flesh. Adam and his wife were both naked, and they felt no shame.

1 Corinthians 7:3–5:

The husband should fulfill his marital duty to his wife, and likewise the wife to her husband... Do not deprive each other except perhaps by mutual consent and for a time, so that you may devote yourselves to prayer.

What does it mean to be "naked and unashamed"—not just physically, but emotionally and spiritually?

Heart-to-Heart Questions

Use these questions to guide your conversation.

1. **Emotional Connection:** What helps us feel close emotionally? What drains that closeness? When was a recent time you felt emotionally connected to me? What made that moment special?
2. **Spiritual Connection:** How would you describe our spiritual life together right now? (Thriving? Surviving? Non-existent?) What would help us grow closer to God together?
3. **Physical Connection:** Is there anything that makes physical intimacy difficult for us right now? How can we create safety in this area? What helps you feel desired? What helps you feel respected?
4. **The Little Foxes:** Hope mentions "the little foxes that ruin the vineyard" (Song of Solomon 2:15). What small distractions have quietly stolen our closeness? (Phones? Busyness? Kids? Work? Exhaustion?) How can we guard against them?
5. **Sacred Rhythms:** What rhythms do we want to implement to strengthen our connection? (Date nights? Prayer times? Screen-free evenings? Morning coffee together? Sabbath rest?)
6. **Affection Inventory:** Small, consistent moments of tenderness matter deeply. What types of affection mean the most to you? How can I show you affection in ways that fill your tank?

Reflection: Our Intimacy Goals

Take turns completing these statements:

"One thing that would help me feel more emotionally connected to you is __________."

"One thing that would help me feel more spiritually connected to you is __________."

"One thing that would help me feel more physically connected to you is __________."

"One rhythm I want us to protect is ________________."

Journaling Prompts

Spend 5–10 minutes journaling individually, then share what you wrote:

- What is my deepest desire for our intimacy?
- What fears or wounds have affected how I connect physically, emotionally, or spiritually?
- What would "naked and unashamed" look like for us in this season?

Going Deeper Exercise: Create Your Rhythms

Together, design rhythms that will protect and strengthen your connection:

- **Daily:** We will connect daily by ____________ (e.g., 10-min conversation, prayer, affection)
- **Weekly:** We will protect weekly connection through ____________________ µ(e.g., date night, Sabbath Evening)
- **Monthly:** We will have a deeper check-in by ____________________
- **Annually:** We will invest in our marriage through ______________________ (e.g., vision retreat, anniversary trip)

This Week's Commitment: Sabbath Evening

Schedule a weekly Sabbath Evening. During this evening, commit together to:

- No screens
- No work
- No heavy or conflict-oriented conversations
- Just connection, tenderness, and play

Our Sabbath Evening will be: Day ___________________ Time ______________

What we will do during our Sabbath Evening: ____________________________

Our Marriage Covenant

Write a brief covenant together—a commitment to pursue healing, wholeness, and holiness:

We, ____________________ and ______________________, commit to:

- ☐ Fight the battle together, not against each other
- ☐ Close the door to secrecy and walk in the light
- ☐ Forgive as Christ has forgiven us

- ☐ Communicate with humility, honesty, and grace
- ☐ Pursue oneness—emotionally, spiritually, and physically
- ☐ Build rhythms that protect and strengthen our marriage
- ☐ Seek help when we need it—from God, from each other, and from wise counsel

Signed: ______________________________ Date: ____________________

Signed: ______________________________ Date: ____________________

Ongoing Rhythms

Commit to these practices going forward:

- Weekly heart check-in: Day ________________ Time ______________
- Nightly questions: "Did I live in the light?" and "How can I serve you?"
- Truth + Grace Table: Day __________________ Time ______________
- Sabbath Evening: Day _______________ Time ______________
- Date night: Day ______________ Frequency ________________
- Prayer together: Time _______________ Frequency _______________
- Daily question: "Jesus, what can we do in Your name today?"

Weekly Check-In Questions

Come back to these questions mid-week:

- How did our Sabbath Evening go? What would make it better?
- What "little foxes" tried to steal our connection this week?
- What is one way I saw you pursuing intimacy with me?

Closing: Blessing

Stand facing each other. Hold hands. Pray this blessing over each other, taking turns:

> *May the Lord bless you and keep you. May He make His face shine upon you and be gracious to you. May He turn His face toward you and give you peace. May your marriage be a place of healing, wholeness, and holiness. May our home be a testimony to the world of what covenant love looks like. In Jesus' name, Amen.*

Be made whole.

Your marriage is worth fighting for.

Group Participant Guide

Group Guidelines

How to Use This Guide

Welcome to the *Made Whole* group participant guide. This four-session course is designed to help couples pursue purity, rebuild trust, strengthen intimacy, and walk in holiness—together.

Each session includes:

- **Opening Prayer**—A suggested prayer to begin your time together
- **Icebreaker**—A question to help everyone connect
- **Key Scripture**—The biblical foundation for the session
- **Video Teaching Notes**—Space to capture key points from the teaching
- **Discussion Questions**—Questions for group conversation
- **Group Activity**—A practical exercise to do together
- **Application**—Practical steps to apply what you have learned
- **Closing Prayer**—A prayer to end your session
- **Going Deeper**—Additional resources for further study
- **Between Sessions Homework**—Work to complete before the next meeting

Group Guidelines

1. **Confidentiality**—What is shared in the group stays in the group. This is essential for creating safety.
2. **Respect**—Listen without judgment. Everyone's journey is different. Avoid giving unsolicited advice.
3. **Participation**—Share openly, but do not dominate the conversation. Make space for quieter voices.
4. **Grace**—Extend grace to one another. We are all works in progress. No one has "arrived."
5. **Commitment**—Prioritize attendance and come prepared. Your presence matters to the group.

Group Participant Session 1

The War for Holiness

"Put on the full armor of God, so that you can take your stand against the devil's schemes."

—Ephesians 6:11

Opening Prayer

Father, as we begin this journey together, open our hearts to receive Your Word. Help us to recognize the battle we are in—not against each other, but against an enemy who wants to destroy our marriages. Give us courage to be honest and grace to support one another. Unite us as we fight for our marriages together. In Jesus' name, Amen.

Icebreaker

If your marriage had a "battle station" to fight against the enemy's attacks, what would be in it? (Prayer? Accountability? Scripture? Community? Something else?) Share with the group.

Key Scripture: Ephesians 6:11–12

Put on the full armor of God, so that you can take your stand against the devil's schemes. For our struggle is not against flesh and blood, but against the rulers, against the authorities, against the powers of this dark world and against the spiritual forces of evil in the heavenly realms.

Video Teaching Notes

Use this space to capture key points from the teaching:

Discussion Questions

1. Joshua says, "Every marriage today is living inside a spiritual war zone—not a war between husband and wife, but a war targeted at husband and wife." How does this perspective change the way you view struggles in your marriage?
2. Hope explains that the enemy's strategy is to "distort our desires, plant deception, create distance, and replace unity with secrecy." Where do you see these tactics at work in marriages today?
3. The teaching describes the anatomy of lust as: desire → deception → disconnection. How does understanding this pattern help us fight more effectively?
4. Joshua teaches that "secrecy is the oxygen of sexual sin." Why is transparency so important in fighting this battle? What makes transparency so difficult?
5. What practical steps from the "battle plan" stood out to you most? What would be most helpful for your marriage right now?
6. Hope reminds us that "Jesus is always stronger than the attack." What does it mean to you that the victory is already secured in Christ?

Group Activity (10 minutes)

In pairs (with your spouse), discuss and write down:

- One digital boundary we want to establish: ________________
- One way we can increase transparency: ___________________
- One person who could be an accountability partner: ______________

Share one insight with the group (as you are comfortable).

Application: This Week's Challenge

- **Digital Boundary:** Establish one new digital boundary in your home this week.
- **Weekly Check-In:** Schedule a time to ask each other: "How are you doing emotionally?" "Where are you feeling tempted?" "How can I pray for you?"
- **Prayer:** Pray together daily: "Lord, help us fight this battle together. Protect our marriage."
- **Accountability:** Identify one trusted, same-sex person who can be an outside accountability partner.

Closing Prayer

Lord, thank You for equipping us to fight this battle. Help us to acknowledge the reality of spiritual warfare. Give us wisdom to build boundaries that protect our marriages. Teach us to fight together—not against each other, but with each other. We trust that in Christ, the victory is already won. In Jesus' name, Amen.

Going Deeper

- Read Ephesians 6:10–18 and identify each piece of the armor of God. Which piece do you need most right now?
- Memorize 1 Corinthians 10:13 this week.
- Read 1 Peter 5:8–9 and reflect on what it means to "resist" the enemy.
- For more resources, visit XOMarriage.com.

Between Sessions Homework

- Complete Couple's Session 1 with your spouse.
- Establish at least one new digital boundary in your home.
- Identify and reach out to a potential accountability partner.
- Begin a daily prayer together: "Lord, protect our marriage."

Group Participant Session 2

The Gospel and the Wounds of Betrayal

"Create in me a pure heart, O God, and renew a steadfast spirit within me. Restore to me the joy of your salvation."

—Psalm 51:10, 12

Opening Prayer

Heavenly Father, we come to You as broken people who have hurt and been hurt. Thank You that the gospel does not just expose sin—it heals the wounds that sin created. Help us to find hope in Your redemption. Give us soft hearts to receive Your truth. In Jesus' name, Amen.

Icebreaker

Think of a time when something broken was restored—a relationship, an object, or a situation. What made that restoration possible? Share briefly with the group.

Key Scripture: 2 Corinthians 7:10

Godly sorrow brings repentance that leads to salvation and leaves no regret, but worldly sorrow brings death.

Video Teaching Notes

Key insights from the teaching:

____

____

____

____

____

____

____

____

____

____

Discussion Questions

1. Joshua says, "Before God restores a marriage, He restores a person." Why is personal heart transformation essential before marital restoration can happen?
2. What is the difference between worldly sorrow and godly repentance? How can you tell the difference in real life?
3. Hope teaches that trust is rebuilt through four stages: Honesty → Consistency → Safety → Intimacy. Which stage do you think is most challenging? Why?
4. Joshua says, "The depth of your confession determines the depth of your healing." What does this mean practically?
5. Hope says, "Boundaries are not bitterness. Forgiveness and boundaries can exist together." How does this truth bring freedom?
6. Joshua reminds us that "intensity does not rebuild trust—consistency rebuilds trust." Why is this distinction important?

Group Activity (10 minutes)

With your spouse, quietly discuss:

- Where are we in the four stages of rebuilding trust? (Honesty → Consistency → Safety → Intimacy)
- What is one thing that would help us move to the next stage?

Share one general insight with the group (nothing too personal).

Application: This Week's Challenge

- **Truth + Grace Table:** Set aside time this week to share one truth and one grace with each other.
- **Scripture Meditation:** Meditate on Psalm 51 this week. Ask God to create a pure heart in you.
- **Daily Prayer:** Pray together: *"Lord, restore to us the joy of Your salvation."*
- **Consistency Inventory:** Ask yourself: *"Am I being consistent in my words, actions, and follow-through?"*

Closing Prayer

Lord, thank You that You do not condemn us—You restore us. Thank You that confession can be the beginning of healing. Help us to practice godly repentance. Rebuild what sin has broken. Give us patience for the process and hope for the journey. In Jesus' name, Amen.

Going Deeper

- Read Psalm 51 in its entirety. Journal your own prayer of repentance.
- Read the story of the woman caught in adultery in John 8:1–11.
- Memorize 2 Corinthians 7:10 this week.
- For more resources, visit XOMarriage.com.

Between Sessions Homework

- Complete Couple's Session 2 with your spouse.
- Practice the Truth + Grace Table at least once this week.
- Read Psalm 51 and journal your response.
- Ask yourself daily: "Am I practicing godly repentance or worldly sorrow?"

Group Participant Session 3

Covenant Forgiveness and Communication

"Be kind and compassionate to one another, forgiving each other, just as in Christ God forgave you."

—Ephesians 4:32

Opening Prayer

Father, we come to You asking for soft hearts. Help us to forgive as You have forgiven us. Teach us to communicate with humility and grace. Where walls have been built, tear them down. Where patterns have been destructive, give us new ways. Make us quick to listen, slow to speak, and slow to become angry. In Jesus' name, Amen.

Icebreaker

What is one communication habit you have seen in healthy relationships? (This could be from your parents, friends, mentors, or others.) Share with the group.

Key Scripture: James 1:19

"Everyone should be quick to listen, slow to speak and slow to become angry."

Video Teaching Notes

Key insights from the teaching:

Discussion Questions

1. Joshua says, "Forgiveness is the doorway through which true communication can walk." Why must forgiveness come before healthy communication?
2. Hope teaches that "forgiveness is a decision; healing is a process." How does understanding this distinction bring freedom?
3. James 1:19 says to be "quick to listen, slow to speak, slow to become angry." Why is listening without defending so difficult?
4. The teaching describes a confession framework: facts first, emotions second, plan for change last. Why is this order important?
5. Joshua says, "Empathy creates emotional safety." How have you experienced this in your own relationships?
6. Hope describes "truth rhythms"—regular practices of confession, gratitude, prayer, and affirmation. Why are rhythms more powerful than one-time conversations?

Group Activity (10 minutes)

With your spouse, practice a "listening without defending" exercise:

- Spouse A shares one thing they appreciate about Spouse B (1 minute).
- Spouse B responds only with: "Thank you. Tell me more about that."
- Switch roles.
- Debrief with the group: What was it like to simply listen and receive?

Application: This Week's Challenge

- **Nightly Practice:** Each night, ask: "Did I live in the light today?" and "How can I serve you tomorrow?"
- **Listening Challenge:** Practice listening without defending. Respond first with: "Help me understand..."
- **Gratitude:** Each day, tell your spouse one specific thing you are grateful for.
- **Empathy Practice:** When your spouse shares a struggle, say: "I am present in your pain with you."

Closing Prayer

Lord, soften our hearts to forgive. Open our ears to truly listen. Guard our tongues to speak truth with grace. Help us build truth rhythms in our marriages. May empathy rebuild what defensiveness has torn down. In Jesus' name, Amen.

Going Deeper

- Read Colossians 3:12-17 and identify the characteristics of healthy relationships.
- Memorize Ephesians 4:32 this week.
- Read Proverbs 18:13 and reflect on what it means to answer before listening.
- For more resources, visit XOMarriage.com.

Between Sessions Homework

- Complete Couple's Session 3 with your spouse.
- Begin the nightly practice: "Did I live in the light?" and "How can I serve you?"
- Practice listening without defending at least three times this week.
- Express gratitude to your spouse daily.

Group Participant Session 4

Redeemed Intimacy

"The two will become one flesh. So they are no longer two, but one flesh."

—Mark 10:8

Opening Prayer

Father, You designed intimacy. You called it good. But life has stolen what You intended to be beautiful. Redeem our intimacy—emotionally, spiritually, and physically. Help us pursue oneness even in the midst of chaos. Heal what has been broken. Restore what has been lost. In Jesus' name, Amen.

Icebreaker

What is the "soundtrack" of your home? Is it busy? Quiet? Full of laughter? Tension? What would you want it to be? Share briefly with the group.

Key Scripture: 1 Corinthians 7:3-5

"The husband should fulfill his marital duty to his wife, and likewise the wife to her husband... Do not deprive each other except perhaps by mutual consent and for a time, so that you may devote yourselves to prayer."

Video Teaching Notes

Key insights from the teaching:

____

____

____

____

____

____

____

____

____

____

Discussion Questions

1. Joshua teaches that "sex is not recreational or transactional—it is covenantal." How does this perspective change the way we approach intimacy?
2. Hope says, "Couples cannot leapfrog emotional intimacy." Why is emotional connection essential before physical intimacy can thrive?
3. The teaching warns about "the little foxes that ruin the vineyard." What are some little foxes that quietly steal intimacy in marriages?
4. Joshua says, "Healthy marriages are not built accidentally. They are built intentionally." What rhythms have you found helpful in building connection?
5. Hope reminds us that "affection is oxygen"—small, consistent moments of tenderness matter. What types of affection are most meaningful to you?
6. As we conclude this course, what is one thing God has spoken to you that you do not want to forget?

Group Activity (15 minutes)

With your spouse, create a brief "Rhythms Plan" for your marriage:

- Daily rhythm we will protect: ______________________
- Weekly rhythm we will protect: ______________________
- One "little fox" we will guard against: ______________________

Share your plans with the group for encouragement and accountability.

Application: Ongoing Rhythms

- **Sabbath Evening:** Schedule a weekly evening with no screens, no work—just connection.
- **Date Nights:** Protect a consistent weekly or bi-weekly date night.
- **Daily Affection:** Small, consistent moments of tenderness—touch, words, eye contact.
- **Spiritual Unity:** Pray together, attend church together, serve together.
- **Weekly Check-In:** Continue the heart check-in: "How are you doing?" "Where are you tempted?"

Closing Prayer

Father, thank You for every marriage in this group. Thank You for Your faithfulness through every chapter of our stories. Lord Jesus, heal what has been broken. Restore what has been lost. Redeem our intimacy—emotionally, spiritually, and physically. May our marriages become places of healing, wholeness, and holiness. May our homes be testimonies to the world of what covenant love looks like. In Jesus' name, Amen.

Going Deeper

- Read Song of Solomon 2:15 and identify the "little foxes" in your marriage.
- Read 1 Corinthians 7:1–5 together as a couple.
- Memorize Mark 10:8–9 this week.
- For more resources, visit XOMarriage.com.

Between Sessions Homework

- Complete Couple's Session 4 with your spouse.
- Schedule your first Sabbath Evening.
- Sign your Marriage Covenant together.
- Commit to your ongoing rhythms and put them on the calendar.

Your marriage was not designed just to survive. In Christ, it was designed to thrive.

Group Participant Appendix

Supporting Group Members in Crisis

As a small group studying marriage, you may encounter members who are experiencing significant marital distress, betrayal, or crisis. Here are resources to help support them:

How to Support Someone in Crisis

- Listen without judgment. Do not rush to fix or offer advice.
- Do not offer simplistic solutions. Avoid platitudes like "Just pray harder."
- Point them toward professional help when needed.
- Remind them of their identity in Christ.
- Stay connected—do not abandon them.
- Pray with them and for them.

Keep crisis resource information handy:

- National Suicide Prevention Lifeline: 988
- Crisis Text Line: Text HOME to 741741
- National Domestic Violence Hotline: 1-800-799-7233
- SAMHSA Helpline (Substance Abuse): 1-800-662-4357

For more resources, visit XOMarriage.com.

Group Leader Guide

Introduction

A Word to Leaders from Joshua & Hope

Welcome, Leader!

Thank you for stepping up to lead a *Made Whole* group. You are about to guide couples through a transformative journey toward healing, wholeness, and holiness in their marriages.

This guide is designed to equip you with everything you need: session-by-session facilitation tips, guidance for handling sensitive topics, and resources for group members who may be struggling.

Because of the nature of this content—sexual purity, betrayal, and rebuilding trust—you will need to lead with extra care, wisdom, and sensitivity. This is sacred ground. Tread carefully, but do not be afraid. God will equip you for what He has called you to.

Your Role as Leader

As a small group leader, you are:

- **A facilitator, not an expert.** You do not need to have all the answers. Your job is to guide discussion, not teach therapy.
- **A shepherd, not a counselor.** You care for people and point them to help when needed, but you are not expected to solve deep-seated issues.
- **A fellow traveler.** You are on this journey too. Be authentic about your own struggles—within appropriate boundaries.
- **A prayer warrior.** Pray for your group members by name throughout the week.
- **A safe person.** People will share things they have never told anyone. Honor that trust. Never gossip.

How to Launch Your Group

1. Pray. Ask God to bring the right couples and prepare hearts.
2. Set the details. Choose a location, day, time, and duration. 90 minutes per session works well.
3. Invite intentionally. Personal invitations work best. Aim for 4-8 couples.
4. Prepare materials. Ensure everyone has access to the video content and study guides.
5. Create a welcoming environment. Comfortable seating, minimal distractions, tissues available.
6. Plan for childcare if needed. This removes a barrier for young families.
7. Coordinate with your church's pastoral staff. Let them know you are leading this group.

Before Your First Session

1. Pray for each couple who will attend.
2. Watch all four video sessions yourself.
3. Review this entire Leader Guide.
4. Prepare your space—comfortable seating, tissues available, good lighting.
5. Have copies of the participant guide for each couple.
6. Have crisis resources readily available (see appendix).

Session Structure (90 minutes suggested)

- Welcome & Opening Prayer: 5 minutes
- Icebreaker: 10 minutes
- Video Teaching: 25–30 minutes
- Group Discussion: 25–30 minutes
- Group Activity: 10 minutes
- Application & Closing Prayer: 10–15 minutes

Facilitation Best Practices

Creating a Safe Environment

- **Establish confidentiality** in Session 1 and reinforce it each week.
- **Model vulnerability.** Share appropriately from your own journey—within boundaries.
- **Never force sharing.** Say, "Share as you feel comfortable."
- **Affirm vulnerability.** When someone shares something hard, thank them.
- **Normalize struggle.** Remind the group: *"You are not alone."*

Managing Discussion

- **Ask open-ended questions.** "What stood out to you?" instead of "Did you like it?"
- **Embrace silence.** Wait 10–15 seconds after asking a question.
- **Redirect dominators.** "Thanks. Let's hear from someone who hasn't shared yet."
- **Draw out the quiet.** "Sarah, any thoughts you'd like to share?"
- **Stay on track.** Gently redirect tangents.
- **Watch the clock.** Do not let one question consume all the time.

Handling Sensitive Moments

- **When someone cries:** Offer tissues, say "Take your time," and let them have the moment.
- **When conflict surfaces between spouses:** Gently say, "This sounds like something important to continue privately."
- **When someone shares abuse or danger:** Take it seriously. Connect them with help immediately.
- **When someone shares something shocking:** Keep your composure. Simply say, "Thank you for trusting us."

Troubleshooting Common Group Dynamics

The Silent Couple

Signs: They attend but rarely share. They look uncomfortable when called on.

Response: Don't pressure them publicly. Check in privately: "I noticed you've been quiet. Is everything okay? Is there anything I can do to help you feel more comfortable?" Offer low-risk opportunities to share.

The Dominating Couple

Signs: They share extensively, interrupt others, or steer every conversation to their story.

Response: Thank them for sharing, then redirect: "Great insight! Let's hear from someone who hasn't shared yet." If it continues, speak privately: "I appreciate your openness. Can you help me draw out some of the quieter couples?"

The Couple in Crisis

Signs: Visible tension between them. One or both seem emotionally fragile. They mention serious issues.

Response: Don't try to counsel them in the group. Meet privately: "I care about you both. What you're facing may need more support than this group can provide. Can I help connect you with some resources?"

The Spouse-Blamer

Signs: They share in ways that make their spouse look bad. "Well, if she would just..." "He never..."

Response: Gently redirect: "Let's focus on our own patterns rather than our spouse's." If it continues, speak privately.

The Advice-Giver

Signs: They try to fix everyone else's problems. "What you should do is..."

Response: Thank them for caring, then redirect: "This group is more about support than solutions. Let's give [couple] space to process."

When to Refer to Professionals

Some situations require more than a small group can provide. Refer couples to professional help when you see:

1. **Any mention of abuse** (physical, emotional, sexual). Safety is the priority.
2. **Addiction issues** (substance, pornography, gambling). Professional treatment is usually needed.
3. **Infidelity.** A trained counselor can help navigate the complex healing process.
4. **Separation or divorce proceedings.** Professional intervention may be needed.
5. **Mental health concerns** (depression, anxiety, suicidal thoughts). These require professional care.
6. **Ongoing, intense conflict** that doesn't respond to the tools in this course.

A Word About Divorce and Separation

Some people engaging with this material are in beautiful seasons of marriage, and some are barely holding on. Some may be separated. Some may be grieving a marriage that has been deeply wounded or has already ended.

If someone in your group is walking through divorce or separation, remember: your role is not to judge or fix. It is to love. Point them toward resources that can help. Remind them that God's grace is sufficient. And walk alongside them with compassion.

Helpful things to say:

- "I'm so sorry you're walking through this. How can I support you?"
- "You are not alone. This group is here for you."
- "God's grace is sufficient, even in this."

Things to avoid:

- "Everything happens for a reason."
- "God hates divorce." (While biblically true, this is not helpful in the moment.)
- "Have you tried...?" (Unsolicited advice)

Group Leader Session 1

The War for Holiness

Key Themes

- The spiritual battle targeting marriage
- The enemy's strategy: distort desires, plant deception, create distance, replace unity with secrecy
- The anatomy of lust: desire → deception → disconnection
- Building a battle plan: honesty → holiness → healthy habits
- The victory is already secured in Christ

Leader Tips

- This is your foundation-setting session. Spend extra time on group guidelines and confidentiality.
- The content may feel confronting. Emphasize grace and hope throughout.
- Watch for couples who seem uncomfortable. Plan to check in privately.
- Normalize the struggle: "This is a battle every marriage faces."
- Be prepared for people to want to talk privately after the session.

Potential Sensitivities

Some participants may be currently struggling with pornography or sexual sin. Others may have recently discovered a spouse's struggle. Be aware that:

- Wives may feel triggered, blamed, or like they are "not enough."
- Husbands may feel exposed, ashamed, or defensive.
- Both may feel hopeless if they have been fighting alone for years.

Helpful phrase: "This course is not about shame. It is about healing. And in Christ, the victory is already secured."

Group Leader Session 2

The Gospel and the Wounds of Betrayal

Key Themes

- Heart transformation before behavioral change
- Worldly sorrow vs. godly repentance
- Confession as restoration, not destruction
- The four stages of rebuilding trust: Honesty → Consistency → Safety → Intimacy
- Boundaries are not bitterness

Leader Tips

- This session can surface deep hurts. Have tissues available.
- Do not let the discussion become a "confession session" where spouses air grievances publicly.
- If someone shares about betrayal, affirm their courage and suggest private follow-up.
- Emphasize that healing is a process, not a one-time event.

Potential Sensitivities

This session may surface significant marital pain. Be aware that:

- Some couples may be in the midst of betrayal discovery—they are raw.
- Some may feel hopeless about ever rebuilding trust.
- Some may feel pressure to forgive before they are ready.

Helpful phrase: "Boundaries are not bitterness. Forgiveness is a decision. Healing is a process."

Group Leader Session 3

Covenant Forgiveness and Communication

Key Themes

- Forgiveness opens the door; communication rebuilds trust
- Listening before defending
- Confession framework: facts first, emotions second, plan for change last
- Truth rhythms: confession, gratitude, prayer, affirmation
- Empathy rewires safety

Leader Tips

- This session is more practical. Help couples see they can implement these ideas today.
- Model good listening during discussion.
- The nightly practice is simple but powerful. Encourage couples to actually try it.
- Consider doing a brief role-play demonstration of good listening vs. defensive listening.

Potential Sensitivities

Some couples may struggle with communication patterns deeply rooted in their family of origin:

- Some may feel defensive when discussing communication struggles.
- Some may feel like they have "tried everything."
- Some may need professional help beyond what a small group can offer.

Helpful phrase: "Communication is hard. But humility and practice can transform how we connect."

Group Leader Session 4

Redeemed Intimacy

Key Themes

- Intimacy is emotional, spiritual, and physical oneness
- Sex is covenantal, not recreational or transactional
- Emotional connection is the soil; physical intimacy is the fruit
- The "little foxes" that steal intimacy
- Sacred rhythms for connection

Leader Tips

This is your closing session. Make it celebratory and hopeful.

- Give time for couples to share what God has done over the four weeks.
- The "Sabbath Evening" challenge is practical. Encourage couples to schedule it before leaving.
- Discuss next steps. Will the group continue? How can you stay connected?
- Consider having a small celebration—desserts, fellowship after the session.

Potential Sensitivities

Discussions about intimacy can be sensitive:

- Some couples may have significant disconnection in this area.
- Some may feel discouraged that they have not "arrived" after four sessions.
- Some may have trauma that affects physical intimacy.

Helpful phrase: "Your marriage was not designed just to survive. In Christ, it was designed to thrive."

Recommended Resources

XO Marriage Resources:

- Free relationship assessments at xomarriage.com
- Marriage coaching and counseling referrals
- Marriage intensives for couples in crisis
- Events and conferences

Counseling Referrals:

- Focus on the Family Counseling: 1-855-771-HELP
- American Association of Christian Counselors: aacc.net

Crisis Hotlines:

- National Domestic Violence Hotline: 1-800-799-7233
- National Suicide Prevention Lifeline: 988
- Crisis Text Line: Text HOME to 741741
- SAMHSA Helpline (Substance Abuse): 1-800-662-4357

Local Resources:

Fill in before your first session:

Your Church's Counseling Ministry: ____________________

Pastoral Contact: ____________________

Christian Counselor 1: ____________________ Phone: ____________________

Christian Counselor 2: ____________________ Phone: ____________________

Appendix A

The Anatomy of Lust

Lust follows a predictable pattern:

DESIRE → DECEPTION → DISCONNECTION

- **Desire:** God-given desire becomes disordered when not surrendered to Christ.
- **Deception:** "No one will know." "It's not a big deal." "I could stop if I wanted."
- **Disconnection:** From God, from spouse, from self.

The path to restoration:

HONESTY → HOLINESS → HEALTHY HABITS

Appendix B

The Four Stages of Rebuilding Trust

1. **HONESTY:** Everything must be brought into the light. No minimizing. No selective storytelling.
2. **CONSISTENCY:** Trust is rebuilt by daily faithful actions. Not intensity—consistency.
3. **SAFETY:** The betrayed spouse must feel safe asking questions without being shamed.
4. **INTIMACY:** Emotional closeness returns before physical closeness. Unity grows slowly.

Key Truth: "Intensity does not rebuild trust. Consistency rebuilds trust."

Appendix C

Truth Rhythms

Build these rhythms into your marriage:

- **CONFESSION:** Proactive honesty before crisis demands it.
- **GRATITUDE:** Specific thankfulness expressed daily.
- **PRAYER:** Regular time praying together.
- **AFFIRMATION:** Words of life, not criticism.
- **BOUNDARIES:** Adjusted and reinforced as needed.

Nightly Questions:

- "Did I live in the light today?"
- "How can I serve you tomorrow?"

A Final Word to Group Leaders

Thank you for investing in the marriages in your group. The work you are doing matters—not just for these couples, but for their children, their churches, and their communities.

Remember: You do not have to be a perfect leader to be an effective one.

Show up. Pray hard. Trust God to do the work that only He can do.

And do not forget to care for your own marriage in the process. You cannot pour from an empty cup.

"Your marriage was not designed just to survive. In Christ, it was designed to thrive."

Healing is available.

Wholeness is possible.

Holiness is worth pursuing.

Intimacy can be redeemed.

For more resources, visit XOMarriage.com.

www.ingramcontent.com/pod-product-compliance
Lightning Source LLC
LaVergne TN
LVHW081325110826
845149LV00007B/1602